Quick & Cute
CARVING PROJECTS

Patterns for **46** Projects
to Carve in One Day

Lori Dickie

WOODCARVING
ILLUSTRATED BOOKS

FOX CHAPEL
PUBLISHING

DEDICATION

I would like to dedicate this book to the people who helped make carving such a large part of my life: my dad, who gave me artistic ability and inspired me with his own talent and works of art; my mom, who thinks everything I do is wonderful, which motivates me to keep trying new things; and my husband, Steve, who encourages and supports me in all that I do, even if it involves trillions of woodchips ... everywhere!

To learn more about the other great books from Fox Chapel Publishing, or to find a retailer near you, call toll-free 800-457-9112 or visit us at *www.FoxChapelPublishing.com*.

Printed in Singapore
First printing

INTRODUCTION

Lori Dickie (right) with her sister, Kristie.

Many years ago, my dad, brother, and sister took up carving. I was afraid of "playing with knives" so I stuck to working with clay. When my dad passed away, my sister, Kristie, talked me into going to the local carving club so we could spend some sisterly time together. I agreed, but I was still nervous about using knives.

The first time I attempted to carve a piece of wood, Kristie's only instruction was to "round" it. I had no idea what to do, and I learned very quickly that once you accidentally remove a large chunk of wood, it might be "game over." Sometimes you can do something tricky to fix it, but it takes a lot of practice to learn to carve with the grain of the wood so you don't accidentally lop off something important. (I also learned that you don't panic and throw your knife when you cut yourself, because you may stab your sister.) I pretty much hated carving, was very frustrated, and decided that I would quit and go back to clay while I still had all of my digits.

That's when my brother, Bill, gave me a basswood egg and a step-by-step book on how to carve a little bird. I was hooked and made a hundred birds. I got better and better at it and gained the confidence to try new characters out of eggs. I discovered that I could purchase other shapes of basswood turnings online and that a variety of patterns were available for them. After that, I let my imagination go crazy, and I started to develop and create my own characters. I don't think a day goes by that I don't get another idea to try.

The turnings that I use most often are basswood eggs in different sizes and a Santa-shaped turning. I have included in this book patterns and step-by-step instructions that show the simple tools and techniques that I use to create an array of different carvings from these two turnings. I have included the colors and brands of paints that I used for each project and tips that may help. I hope others have as much fun as I do carving these characters and, because the turnings are "rounded" and the designs are simple, even beginners can be successful and perhaps find a new passion in carving.

Lori's dad, Tom Bowman, started the family's carving tradition.

CONTENTS

Getting Started

Basswood Eggs

My first attempts at carving were very frustrating because I didn't know how to "round" the blank. I only began loving carving after my brother, Bill, gave me a basswood egg blank, which comes pre-rounded. Carving eggs and other turnings lets me skip the confusing part and get straight to the fun: creating the character and adding details.

The eggs I use are turned from basswood, which is a light wood with even grain that is easy to carve. Although you can purchase chunks of basswood from local craft stores, they don't usually carry basswood turnings. The eggs and balls they sell are made of hardwood and are very hard to carve. Instead, I purchase the turnings online from the sources listed below. (Woodworking shows are also a good source of basswood blanks.)

The Woodcraft Shop, 1-800-397-2278, www.thewoodcraftshop.com
- Hen eggs: 2½" (64mm) tall (item 531101)
- Goose eggs: 4" (10.2cm) tall (item 554709)
- Small Santa: 1¾" by 3" (44mm by 76mm) (#2/CHRISTKINDL; item 554731)
- Large Santa: 3½" by 5¾" (89mm by 14.6cm) (#1; item 554703)

Stadtlander Woodcarving Supplies, 1-330-931-7847, www.stadtlandercarvings.com
- Pigeon eggs: 2" (51mm) tall (item #5501)
- Hen eggs: 2¾" (70mm) tall (item # 5502)
- Goose eggs: 3½" (89mm) tall (item #5503)

I use two kinds of turned basswood blanks: eggs and Santas.

You'll need just a handful of tools, including a detail knife with a small blade, micro gouges, and a woodburner.

Basic Tools

I use four tools for all of my carvings: a small carving knife, two miniature carving gouges, and a woodburner. You can get started with just a knife and then try additional tools and decide if you like them.

Knife: Because my carvings are not very large, I use a small detail knife to carve. The blade is about 1¼" (32mm) long. Your knife is always a personal choice based on the knife that feels comfortable in your hand and suits your carving style. Folks with stronger hands use a larger knife and take big "bites" from the wood. I am a nibbler, so a detail knife works better for me.

Sharpening is an art in itself. My friends at the carving club taught me how to sharpen, and I stumble through it each time and somehow end up with a sharp knife. I can't really teach others, but there are books and websites that describe the process in detail. I highly recommend finding instructions or a teacher and learning to sharpen your tools. Not only does a sharp knife make nice clean cuts, but it is much safer to carve with sharp tools.

Micro carving gouges: I use tiny (2mm) U- and V-shaped gouges to make hair, fur, hatbands, etc. They are helpful, but you can use a knife to get the same effects. You can purchase micro gouges from The Woodcraft Shop and Stadtlander Woodcarving Supplies, as well as other tool suppliers. They tend to be sold in sets and can be expensive, so I suggest trying them—borrow them from a friend or try them at a show—before you invest in them.

Woodburner: I like using a woodburner on my carvings because it lets me add a lot more detail. (If you prefer, add the details with paint, instead.) If you try a woodburner, I recommend using one that has adjustable heat and a drawing or writing tip. Although this can be an expensive investment, Walnut Hollow makes an affordable version that's available at craft stores and would let you experiment. Wait to buy a professional burner until you are sure you need it.

Paint and Finish

Paint is another personal choice. I use acrylic paint, and I usually buy the paint that is on sale. I have listed the colors and brands I used on each carving, but any of the all-purpose craft acrylic paints will work.

When I'm painting, I dilute the paint 1:1 with water when I want the carving marks and/or brown woodburning to show. I use the paint full strength if I want the woodburned marks to show, but not the color. For example, if I woodburn curls on a sheep, I want to see the texture but not the brown color, so I cover the curls with full-strength paint.

Here are a few more painting techniques I use on almost every carving.

Drybrushing: Load a brush with a contrasting color and wipe it on a towel until the brush is dry. Brush lightly over the carving to add more detail and bring out the carving marks.

Antiquing: Let the carving dry for several hours. Water down dark brown acrylic paint and paint it all over the carving. Wipe off most of the brown paint with a damp

I paint my carvings with craft acrylics. Any brand will work; I generally buy what's on sale!

cloth, leaving a small amount in the nooks and crannies to create the antique look.

Finish: I finish all of my carvings with water-based, all-purpose, matte-finish varnish. This is sold in craft stores. Use one or two coats to seal the whole carving, and then let it dry overnight.

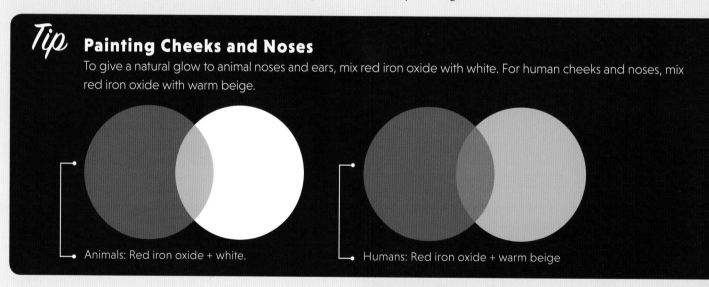

Tip **Painting Cheeks and Noses**

To give a natural glow to animal noses and ears, mix red iron oxide with white. For human cheeks and noses, mix red iron oxide with warm beige.

Animals: Red iron oxide + white.

Humans: Red iron oxide + warm beige

Safety

I recommend that you find a comfortable carving glove and wear it while you work. And, again, learn how to sharpen and strop your tools, and keep them sharp. Sharp tools are actually safer to carve with because you don't need to push them as hard and can control them better.

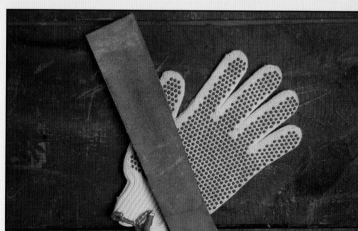

Sharp tools are safer than dull tools, so use a strop often—but wear a glove, too.

Carving Instructions

Carving a Dog: An Egg Blank Tutorial

MATERIALS:

- Basswood egg: hen size
- Graphite paper (optional)
- Paint: brown (3), black (3), white (1), red iron oxide (4)
- Varnish: matte

TOOLS:

- Carving knife
- Woodburner with writing tip (optional)
- Pencil
- Paintbrush

See paint key on page 12.

I use two types of basswood turnings for most of my carvings: the egg shape and the Santa shape. I'm including a step-by-step project for each type of blank. Although the shapes are different, the techniques are the same. Once you do the practice projects, you should be able to generalize the instructions to make any of the projects in this book.

This design was inspired by my dog, Zak, whose happy expression always made me smile. I used a basswood hen's egg. If you want to start with a larger project, choose a basswood goose egg and photocopy the pattern at 160 percent so it will fit the larger blank. The dog can easily be made to look like different breeds by changing the type of ears and the paint color. Display the carving on a shelf or mantle, or add a brass screw eye to the top and use it as an ornament.

Tip Centerlines

A centerline is a line drawn around a project to divide it into halves (usually left and right). I often draw two crossed, vertical centerlines on an egg to divide it into quarters, which helps keep the sides symmetrical.

Making a Stop Cut

Cut straight into the wood with the edge of the blade. You will usually then angle the knife and cut toward the stop cut to remove a chip of wood.

Transferring Patterns

You can photocopy the pattern and use graphite paper to transfer it to the egg, but that's challenging because the surface is round. It's easier to "eyeball" it and sketch the design with a pencil.

DOG: CARVING THE BODY

1

Transfer the pattern to the egg. Draw a vertical centerline on the side of the egg where the grain is straight. Choose one side to be the front of the dog. Draw a second vertical centerline through the center of the front and back. Either sketch the pattern or transfer it using graphite paper. Note: I drew the pattern lines with ink so they are visible in the photos; you should use pencil.

2

Define the neck. With a knife, make stop cuts (see Tip) around the neck line several times until the cut is ¼" (6mm) deep. Then, angle the knife and carve up to the stop cut to remove the wood on both sides of the line. Continue to stop-cut and remove wood until the neck is formed.

3

Define the body. Make stop cuts along the lines for the legs, feet, haunches, and tail. Carve around the legs, tail, haunches, and feet toward the stop cuts to define each feature.

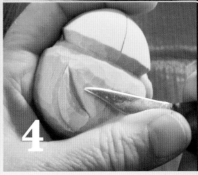

4

Round the body. Round and shape the body, comparing both sides to maintain symmetry. Remove wood all over the body, because uncarved wood will take finish differently than the carved surface.

DOG: CARVING THE HEAD

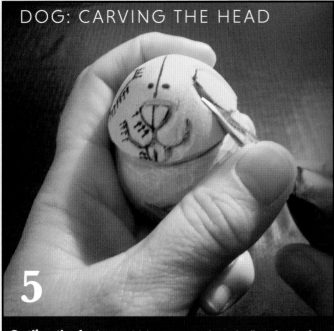

5

Outline the features. Make stop cuts along the lines for the face and ears. Carve around the face and ears toward the stop cuts to define the features.

6

Round the head. Round and shape the head, maintaining symmetry and being sure to carve the entire surface.

7

Form the nose and face. Scoop out the eye area above the nose. Round the face to define the features. Blend the edges of the eye area with the rest of the head.

DOG: COMPLETING THE PROJECT

8

Woodburn the fine details (optional). Using a woodburner with a writing tip, burn along the cuts to remove burrs and add the facial features.

9

Finish the project. Paint the dog a color of your choice; I used brown. Paint the nose black and the tongue red iron oxide mixed with white. For a fur-like effect, drybrush the carving with undiluted white or brown paint to highlight the carved texture. (See page 8 for instructions.) Wait until the paint dries and apply two coats of matte varnish.

PAINT KEY

1 Americana® Acrylics

3 Craft Smart® Acrylic

4 Delta Ceramcoat® Acrylic

Painting Guide:

Eyes: Black (3)

Nose: Black (3)

Tongue: Red iron oxide (4) mixed with white (1)

Fur: Brown (3) diluted 1:1 with water; drybrush with full-strength brown

BACK   FRONT   SIDE

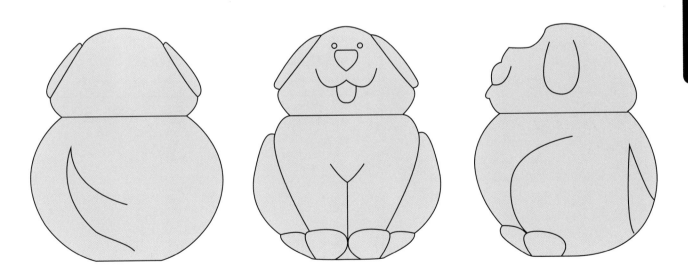

Carving a Snowman: A Santa Blank Tutorial

MATERIALS:
- Basswood Santa: small #2 size (1 ¾" x 3 ⅝", or 44mm x 92mm)
- Graphite paper (optional)
- Paint: bright red (3), white (1), pumpkin (4), black (3), apple tart green (3), Christmas green (2)
- Varnish: matte

See paint key on page 16.

TOOLS:
- Carving knife
- Micro (2mm) V-tool
- Woodburner with writing tip
- Pencil
- Paintbrush

The Santa shape is one of my favorite turned carving blanks. It's shaped like a teardrop with a ridge in the middle, and I use it for all kinds of carvings, including a cow, pig, witch, fairy, pilgrim, and trick-or-treater. I'll show you the basic techniques with this snowman project, and then you can generalize the instructions to make many other characters. I used the small size Santa blank; if you prefer to use the larger size, copy the pattern at 200 percent before transferring it to the wood. See page 66 for the tree pattern.

SNOWMAN: CARVING THE HAT

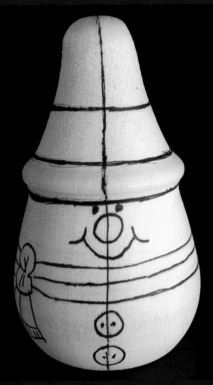

1

Transfer the pattern. Draw a centerline on the side of the turning where the grain is straight. Choose one side to be the front of the snowman. Draw a second vertical centerline through the center of the front and back. Either sketch the pattern or transfer it using graphite paper. Note: I drew the pattern lines with ink so they are visible in the photos; you should use pencil. (See page 10 for information on Centerlines and Transferring Patterns.)

2

Form the top of the hat. Use a knife to make a stop cut around the top line on the hat. (See page 10 for Stop Cut instructions.) Then, angle the knife and carve up to the stop cut to remove wood on both sides of the line. Continue to make stop cuts and remove wood until the cut is ¼" (6mm) deep. Round the top to form a pom-pom.

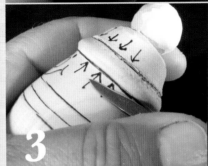

3

Form the hatband. The ridge of the Santa blank will form the hatband. Make stop cuts around the bottom two lines on the hat. Remove wood from above the top line down to the stop cut. Remove wood from below the bottom line up to the stop cut. Carve the hatband flat.

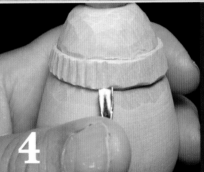

4

Finish carving the hat. Round and shape the hat. Remove the wood all over the hat, because uncarved wood will take finish differently than the carved surface. Use the tip of the knife or a small V-tool to carve grooves in the hatband to resemble ribbing.

SNOWMAN: CARVING THE SCARF, HEAD & BODY

5

Carve the scarf. Make stop cuts along the top and bottom lines of the scarf. Carve toward the stop cuts to define the scarf and to begin to round the head and body. Make stop cuts around the knot and carve up to them to define the knot and separate it from the scarf. Use the tip of the knife to carve a notch at the center of the scarf. Round the scarf, knot, and dangling ends.

6

Carve the head and body. Round them gently, creating even curves all the way around. Remove the wood all over the head and body, because uncarved wood will take finish differently than the carved surface.

SNOWMAN: FINISHING THE PROJECT

7 **Add the features and details.** Redraw the face and buttons. Use a woodburner to draw the face, scarf stripes, buttons, and a design on the hat.

8 **Paint the carving.** Mix acrylic paints 1:1 with water so the woodburned details show through the paint. Paint the snowman as shown in the Painting Guide. Allow the paint to dry, and then seal the carving with two coats of matte varnish.

PAINT KEY

1 - Americana® Acrylics

2 - Apple Barrel® Colors

3 - Craft Smart® Acrylic

4 - Delta Ceramcoat® Acrylic

Painting Guide:

Pom-pom, head, body: White (1)

Hat, buttons: Bright red (3)

Cheeks: Heavily diluted red

Nose: Pumpkin (4)

Hat details, eyes, mouth, and buttonholes: Black (3)

Scarf: Apple tart green (3), Christmas green (2)

FRONT

BACK

SIDE

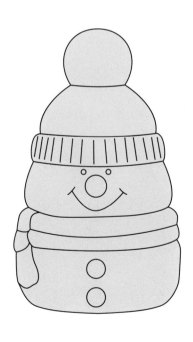
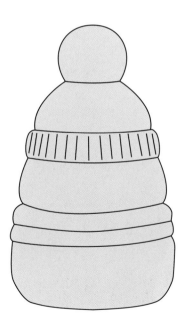
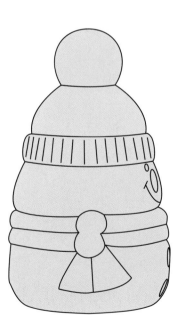

Funny Farm Animals

Paint and Finish

Paint is another personal choice. I use acrylic paint, and I usually buy the paint that is on sale. I have listed the colors and brands I used on each carving, but any of the all-purpose craft acrylic paints will work.

When I'm painting, I dilute the paint 1:1 with water when I want the carving marks and/or brown woodburning to show. I use the paint full strength if I want the woodburned marks to show, but not the color. For example, if I woodburn curls on a sheep, I want to see the texture but not the brown color, so I cover the curls with full-strength paint.

Here are a few more painting techniques I use on almost every carving.

Drybrushing: Load a brush with a contrasting color and wipe it on a towel until the brush is dry. Brush lightly over the carving to add more detail and bring out the carving marks.

Antiquing: Let the carving dry for several hours. Water down dark brown acrylic paint and paint it all over the carving. Wipe off most of the brown paint with a damp

I paint my carvings with craft acrylics. Any brand will work; I generally buy what's on sale!

cloth, leaving a small amount in the nooks and crannies to create the antique look.

Finish: I finish all of my carvings with water-based, all-purpose, matte-finish varnish. This is sold in craft stores. Use one or two coats to seal the whole carving, and then let it dry overnight.

Tip Painting Cheeks and Noses

To give a natural glow to animal noses and ears, mix red iron oxide with white. For human cheeks and noses, mix red iron oxide with warm beige.

Animals: Red iron oxide + white.

Humans: Red iron oxide + warm beige

Safety

I recommend that you find a comfortable carving glove and wear it while you work. And, again, learn how to sharpen and strop your tools, and keep them sharp. Sharp tools are actually safer to carve with because you don't need to push them as hard and can control them better.

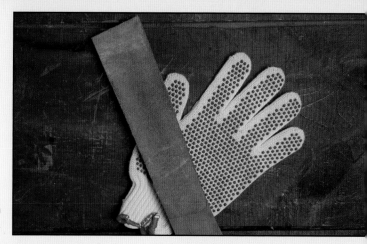

Sharp tools are safer than dull tools, so use a strop often—but wear a glove, too.

Basswood Eggs

My first attempts at carving were very frustrating because I didn't know how to "round" the blank. I only began loving carving after my brother, Bill, gave me a basswood egg blank, which comes pre-rounded. Carving eggs and other turnings lets me skip the confusing part and get straight to the fun: creating the character and adding details.

The eggs I use are turned from basswood, which is a light wood with even grain that is easy to carve. Although you can purchase chunks of basswood from local craft stores, they don't usually carry basswood turnings. The eggs and balls they sell are made of hardwood and are very hard to carve. Instead, I purchase the turnings online from the sources listed below. (Woodworking shows are also a good source of basswood blanks.)

The Woodcraft Shop, 1-800-397-2278, www.thewoodcraftshop.com
- Hen eggs: 2½" (64mm) tall (item 531101)
- Goose eggs: 4" (10.2cm) tall (item 554709)
- Small Santa: 1¾" by 3" (44mm by 76mm) (#2/CHRISTKINDL; item 554731)
- Large Santa: 3½" by 5¾" (89mm by 14.6cm) (#1; item 554703)

Stadtlander Woodcarving Supplies, 1-330-931-7847, www.stadtlandercarvings.com
- Pigeon eggs: 2" (51mm) tall (item #5501)
- Hen eggs: 2¾" (70mm) tall (item # 5502)
- Goose eggs: 3½" (89mm) tall (item #5503)

I use two kinds of turned basswood blanks: eggs and Santas.

You'll need just a handful of tools, including a detail knife with a small blade, micro gouges, and a woodburner.

Basic Tools

I use four tools for all of my carvings: a small carving knife, two miniature carving gouges, and a woodburner. You can get started with just a knife and then try additional tools and decide if you like them.

Knife: Because my carvings are not very large, I use a small detail knife to carve. The blade is about 1¼" (32mm) long. Your knife is always a personal choice based on the knife that feels comfortable in your hand and suits your carving style. Folks with stronger hands use a larger knife and take big "bites" from the wood. I am a nibbler, so a detail knife works better for me.

Sharpening is an art in itself. My friends at the carving club taught me how to sharpen, and I stumble through it each time and somehow end up with a sharp knife. I can't really teach others, but there are books and websites that describe the process in detail. I highly recommend finding instructions or a teacher and learning to sharpen your tools. Not only does a sharp knife make nice clean cuts, but it is much safer to carve with sharp tools.

Micro carving gouges: I use tiny (2mm) U- and V-shaped gouges to make hair, fur, hatbands, etc. They are helpful, but you can use a knife to get the same effects. You can purchase micro gouges from The Woodcraft Shop and Stadtlander Woodcarving Supplies, as well as other tool suppliers. They tend to be sold in sets and can be expensive, so I suggest trying them—borrow them from a friend or try them at a show—before you invest in them.

Woodburner: I like using a woodburner on my carvings because it lets me add a lot more detail. (If you prefer, add the details with paint, instead.) If you try a woodburner, I recommend using one that has adjustable heat and a drawing or writing tip. Although this can be an expensive investment, Walnut Hollow makes an affordable version that's available at craft stores and would let you experiment. Wait to buy a professional burner until you are sure you need it.

Potter the Pig

Painting Guide:

Body: Ballet pink (5)

Hooves: Black (3)

Bandana: White (1), bright red (3)

MATERIALS:

- Basswood Santa: small #2 size (1 ¾" x 3 ⅝", or 44mm x 92mm)
- Graphite paper (optional)
- Paint: ballet pink (5), black (3), white (1), bright red (3)
- Varnish: matte

TOOLS:

- Carving knife
- Woodburner with writing tip
- Pencil
- Paintbrush

PAINT KEY

1 - Americana® Acrylics
2 - Apple Barrel® Colors
3 - Craft Smart® Acrylic
4 - Delta Ceramcoat® Acrylic
5 - FolkArt® Acrylic
6 - DecoArt® Crafter's Acrylic®
7 - FolkArt® Metallics
8 - DecoArt® Dazzling Metallics

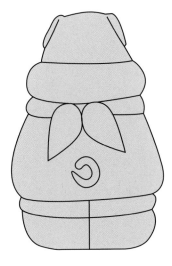

Bessie the Cow

Painting Guide:

Body: White (1)

Spots, hooves: Black (3)

Bell: Metallic gold (4)

Nose, horns: White (1) mixed with red iron oxide (4)

Ribbon: Bright red (3)

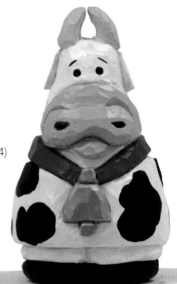

MATERIALS:
- Basswood Santa: small #2 size (1 ¾" x 3 ⅝", or 44mm x 92mm)
- Graphite paper (optional)
- Paint: white (1), black (3), metallic gold (4), bright red (3), red iron oxide (4)
- Varnish: matte

TOOLS:
- Carving knife
- Woodburner with writing tip
- Pencil
- Paintbrush

PAINT KEY

1 - Americana® Acrylics
2 - Apple Barrel® Colors
3 - Craft Smart® Acrylic
4 - Delta Ceramcoat® Acrylic
5 - FolkArt® Acrylic
6 - DecoArt® Crafter's Acrylic®
7 - FolkArt® Metallics
8 - DecoArt® Dazzling Metallics

PATTERNS

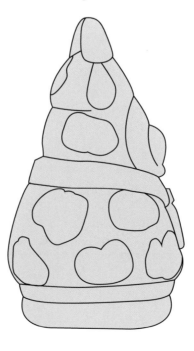

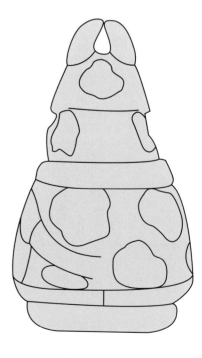

Billy the Goat

Painting Guide:

Body: White (1)

Nose, inner ears: Red iron oxide (4) mixed with white (1)

Horns: Golden brown (3)

Hooves: Black (3)

MATERIALS:
- Basswood Santa: small #2 size (1 ¾" x 3 ⅝", or 44mm x 92mm)
- Graphite paper (optional)
- Paint: black (3), white (1), golden brown (3), red iron oxide (4)
- Varnish: matte

TOOLS:
- Carving knife
- Woodburner with writing tip
- Pencil
- Paintbrush

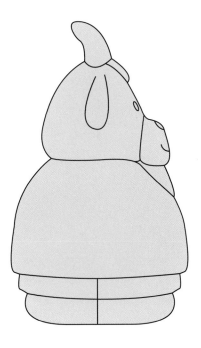

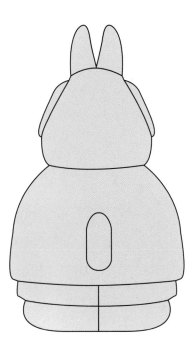

Dixie Chicken

Painting Guide:

Body: White (1)

Comb, wattles: Bright red (3)

Eyes: Black (3)

Beak: Dark yellow (3)

MATERIALS:

- Basswood egg: hen size
- Graphite paper (optional)
- Paint: white (1), black (3), bright red (3), dark yellow (3)
- Varnish: matte

TOOLS:

- Carving knife
- Woodburner with writing tip
- Pencil
- Paintbrush

PAINT KEY

1 - Americana® Acrylics
2 - Apple Barrel® Colors
3 - Craft Smart® Acrylic
4 - Delta Ceramcoat® Acrylic
5 - FolkArt® Acrylic
6 - DecoArt® Crafter's Acrylic®
7 - FolkArt® Metallics
8 - DecoArt® Dazzling Metallics

Use a micro V-tool to carve the pony's mane and tail. When he's not helping out on the farm, the pony would make a good steed for the Knight (page 29).

Pickles the Pony

Painting Guide:

Body: Brown (3)

Mane, tail, hooves: Black (3)

Bridle: Bright red (3)

Muzzle: White (1)

Inner ears: White (1) mixed with red iron oxide (4)

MATERIALS:

- Basswood Santa: small #2 size (1 ¾" x 3 ⅝", or 44mm x 92mm)
- Graphite paper (optional)
- Paint: black (3), white (1), bright red (3), brown (3), warm beige (1), red iron oxide (4)
- Varnish: matte

TOOLS:

- Carving knife
- Micro (2mm) V-tool
- Woodburner with writing tip
- Pencil
- Paintbrush

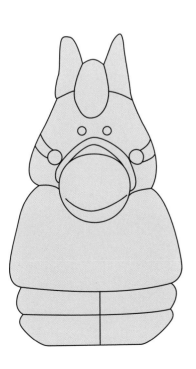

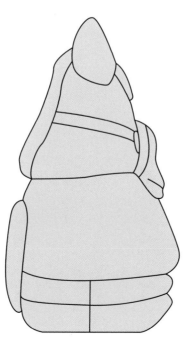

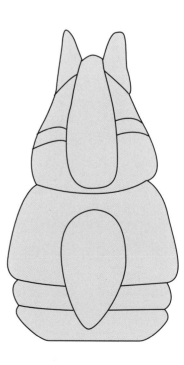

Wooly the Sheep

Tip — Use the woodburner to add swirls for wool.

Painting Guide:

Body, eyes: White (1)

Hooves, face: Black (3)

Nose, inner ears: Red iron oxide (4) mixed with white (1)

MATERIALS:

- Basswood Santa: small #2 size (1 ¾" x 3 ⅝", or 44mm x 92mm)
- Graphite paper (optional)
- Paint: black (3), white (1), red iron oxide (4)
- Varnish: matte

TOOLS:

- Carving knife
- Woodburner with writing tip
- Pencil
- Paintbrush

PAINT KEY

1 - Americana® Acrylics
2 - Apple Barrel® Colors
3 - Craft Smart® Acrylic
4 - Delta Ceramcoat® Acrylic
5 - FolkArt® Acrylic
6 - DecoArt® Crafter's Acrylic®
7 - FolkArt® Metallics
8 - DecoArt® Dazzling Metallics

PATTERNS

Gladys the Goose

Painting Guide:

Body: White (1)

Eyes: Black (3)

Beak, feet: Dark yellow (3)

MATERIALS:

- Basswood Santa: small #2 size (1 ¾" x 3 ⅝", or 44mm x 92mm)
- Graphite paper (optional)
- Paint: black (3), white (1), dark yellow (3)
- Varnish: matte

TOOLS:

- Carving knife
- Woodburner with writing tip
- Pencil
- Paintbrush

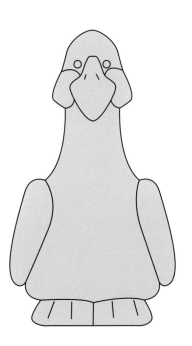

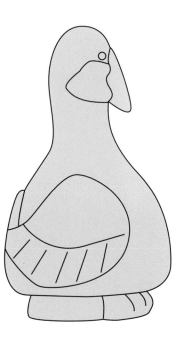

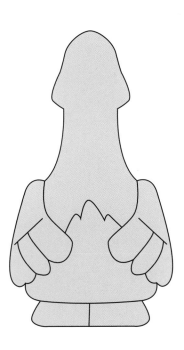

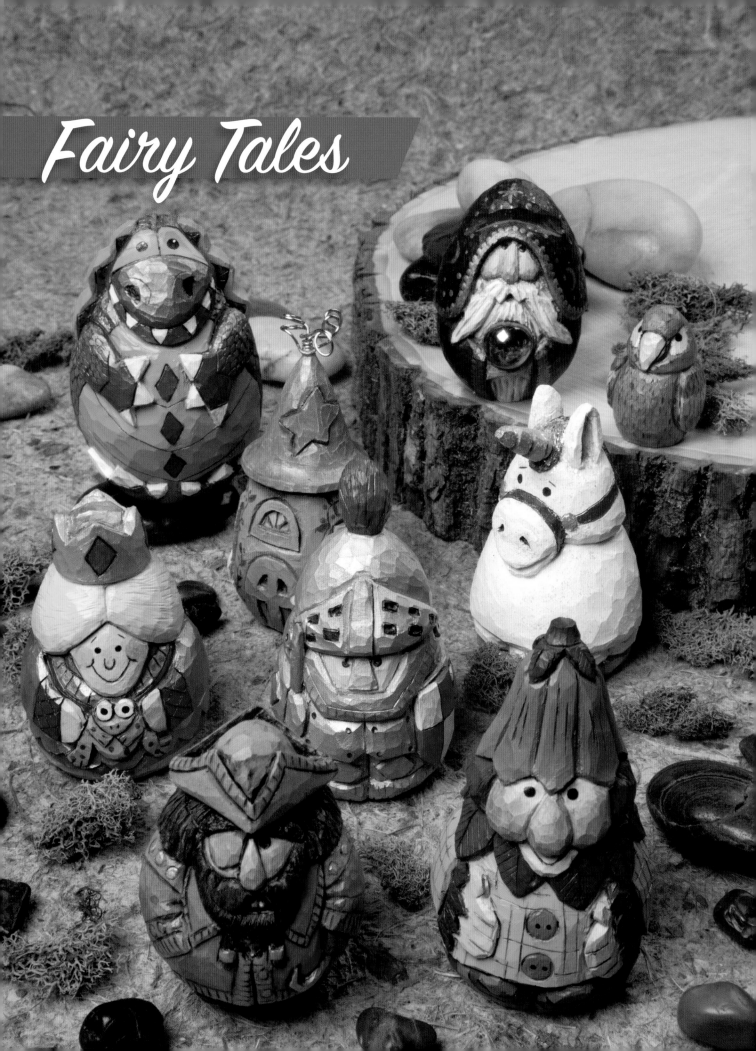

Fairy Tales

Use the micro V-tool to carve the beard. Use a micro U-gouge to carve a hole above the hands. Glue a marble into the hole to serve as a crystal ball.

Painting Guide:

Hat, robe: Metallic black (5)

Trim: Metallic gold (4)

Face, hands: Warm beige (1) mixed with red iron oxide (4)

Beard, mustache: White (1)

Top coat: Glitter glue

MATERIALS:

- Basswood egg: hen size
- Graphite paper (optional)
- Paint: white (1), metallic black (5), metallic gold (4), warm beige (1), red iron oxide (4)
- Varnish: matte
- Cyanoacrylate (CA) glue, such as Super Glue®
- Marble: ½" (13mm) dia.
- Glitter glue

TOOLS:

- Carving knife
- Micro (2mm) V-tool
- Micro (2mm) U-gouge
- Woodburner with writing tip
- Pencil
- Paintbrush

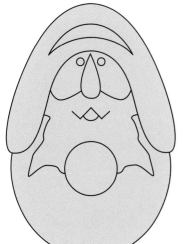

PAINT KEY

1 - Americana® Acrylics
2 - Apple Barrel® Colors
3 - Craft Smart® Acrylic
4 - Delta Ceramcoat® Acrylic
5 - FolkArt® Acrylic
6 - DecoArt® Crafter's Acrylic®
7 - FolkArt® Metallics
8 - DecoArt® Dazzling Metallics

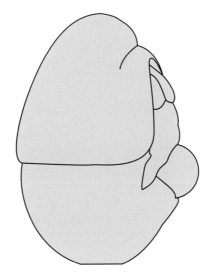

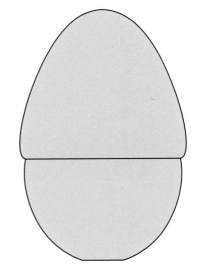

Princess

MATERIALS:

- Basswood Santa: small #2 size (1 ¾" x 3 ⅝", or 44mm x 92mm)
- Graphite paper (optional)
- Paint: white (1), black (3), bright yellow (3), metallic gold (4), aquamarine (7), royal ruby (8), apple tart green (3), white (1), warm beige (1), red iron oxide (4), Christmas green (2)
- Varnish: matte

TOOLS:

- Carving knife
- Woodburner with writing tip
- Pencil
- Paintbrush

PAINT KEY

1 - Americana® Acrylics
2 - Apple Barrel® Colors
3 - Craft Smart® Acrylic
4 - Delta Ceramcoat® Acrylic
5 - FolkArt® Acrylic
6 - DecoArt® Crafter's Acrylic®
7 - FolkArt® Metallics
8 - DecoArt® Dazzling Metallics

PATTERNS

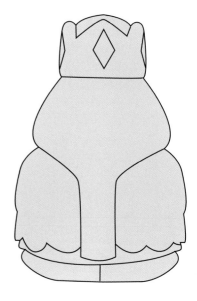

For the spear, shape either a small dowel or a basswood strip, cut it in half, and glue the pieces above and below the hand. Pickles the Pony (page 23) makes a good steed for the Knight.

Knight

Painting Guide:

Armor: Metallic silver (7)

Face: Warm beige (1)

Feather, shield: Bright red (3)

Shield: White (1)

MATERIALS:

- Basswood Santa: small #2 size (1 ¾" x 3 ⅝", or 44mm x 92mm)
- Graphite paper (optional)
- Paint: white (1), black (3), metallic silver (7), warm beige (1), bright red (3)
- Varnish: matte

TOOLS:

- Carving knife
- Woodburner with writing tip
- Pencil
- Paintbrush

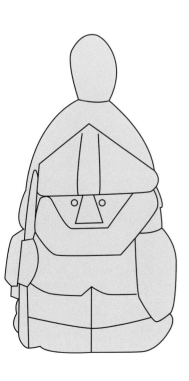

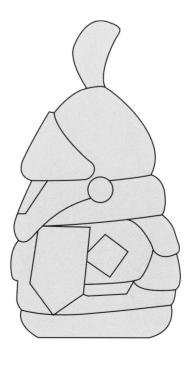

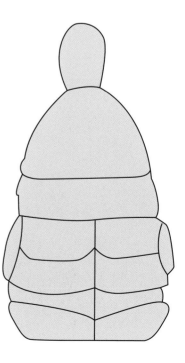

Unicorn

Tip For the horn, carve a small piece of basswood into a cone with spirals and glue it to the forehead.

Painting Guide:

Body: White (1)

Horn, hooves: Metallic gold (4)

Mane, tail: Purple pearl (8)

Eyes, nostrils: Black (3)

Bridle: Metallic solid bronze (7)

Topcoat: Glitter glue

MATERIALS:

- Basswood Santa: small #2 size (1 ¾" x 3 ⅝", or 44mm x 92mm)
- Graphite paper (optional)
- Paint: white (1), metallic gold (4), purple pearl (8), black (3), metallic solid bronze (7)
- Varnish: matte
- Glitter glue
- Cyanoacrylate (CA) glue, such as Super Glue®

TOOLS:

- Carving knife
- Woodburner with writing tip
- Pencil
- Paintbrush

PAINT KEY

1 - Americana® Acrylics
2 - Apple Barrel® Colors
3 - Craft Smart® Acrylic
4 - Delta Ceramcoat® Acrylic
5 - FolkArt® Acrylic
6 - DecoArt® Crafter's Acrylic®
7 - FolkArt® Metallics
8 - DecoArt® Dazzling Metallics

PATTERNS

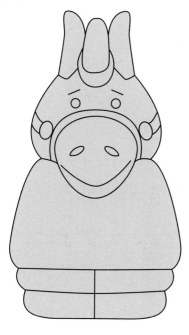

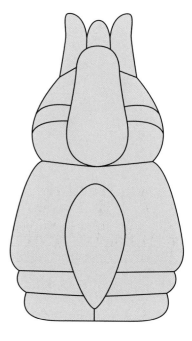

Woodburn small scales on the arms, back, and sides.

Painting Guide:

Eyes, nostrils:
Black (3)

Teeth, claws:
White (1)

Body, face, arms,
tail: Crystal green (8)

Belly, body accents:
Apple tart green (3)

MATERIALS:

- Basswood egg: goose size
- Graphite paper (optional)
- Paint: white (1), black (3), apple tart green (3), crystal green (8)
- Varnish: matte

TOOLS:

- Carving knife
- Woodburner with writing tip
- Pencil
- Paintbrush

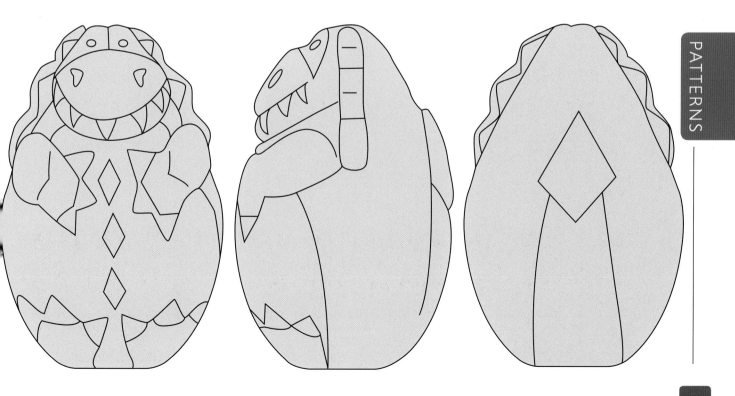

PATTERNS

Pirate

Painting Guide:

Hair, beard, shoes: Black (3)

Coat: Bright red (3)

Coat trim: Deep periwinkle (1)

Face: Warm beige (1) mixed with red iron oxide (4)

Hook: Metallic silver (7)

Buttons: Metallic gold (4)

MATERIALS:

- Basswood Santa (pirate): small #2 size (1 ¾" x 3 ⅝", or 44mm x 92mm)
- Graphite paper (optional)
- Paint: white (1), black (3), deep periwinkle (1), bright red (3), warm beige (1), red iron oxide (4), metallic silver (7), metallic gold (4)
- Varnish: matte

TOOLS:

- Carving knife
- Woodburner with writing tip
- Pencil
- Paintbrush

PAINT KEY

1 - Americana® Acrylics
2 - Apple Barrel® Colors
3 - Craft Smart® Acrylic
4 - Delta Ceramcoat® Acrylic
5 - FolkArt® Acrylic
6 - DecoArt® Crafter's Acrylic®
7 - FolkArt® Metallics
8 - DecoArt® Dazzling Metallics

PATTERNS

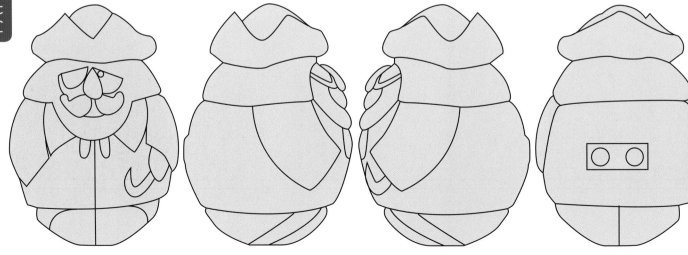

Parrot

Painting Guide:

Eyes, sides of beak: Black (3)

Eyes, beak: White (1)

Body: Bright red (3)

Wings: Deep periwinkle (1), bright yellow (3)

MATERIALS:

- Basswood egg (parrot): pigeon size
- Graphite paper (optional)
- Paint: white (1), black (3), deep periwinkle (1), bright red (3), bright yellow (3)
- Varnish: matte

TOOLS:

- Carving knife
- Woodburner with writing tip
- Pencil
- Paintbrush

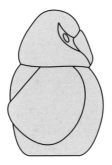

Fairy

Painting Guide:

Face, hands: Warm beige (1) mixed with red iron oxide (4)

Jacket: Gecko (4)

Hat, buttons, shoes: Lavender (1)

Trim: Christmas green (2)

Hair: Brown (3)

Eyes: Black (3)

MATERIALS:

- Basswood Santa: small #2 size (1 ¾" x 3 ⅝", or 44mm x 92mm)
- Graphite paper (optional)
- Paint: warm beige (1), red iron oxide (4), gecko (4), lavender (1), Christmas green (2), brown (3), black (3)
- Varnish: matte

TOOLS:

- Carving knife
- Woodburner with writing tip
- Pencil
- Paintbrush

PAINT KEY

1 - Americana® Acrylics
2 - Apple Barrel® Colors
3 - Craft Smart® Acrylic
4 - Delta Ceramcoat® Acrylic

5 - FolkArt® Acrylic
6 - DecoArt® Crafter's Acrylic®
7 - FolkArt® Metallics
8 - DecoArt® Dazzling Metallics

PATTERNS

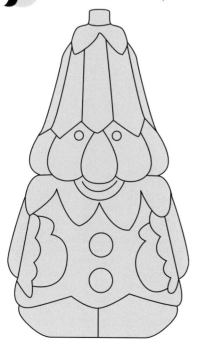

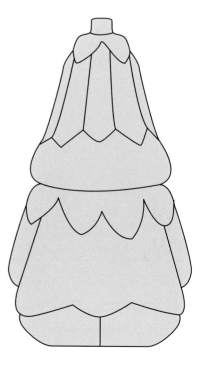

Fairy Cottage

Painting Guide:

House: Lavender (1)

Windows: Bright yellow (3)

Roof: Metallic gold (4)

Trim: White (1)

Flowers: Bright red (3)

Trim: Deep periwinkle (1)

Leaves, vines, roof drybrush: hunter green (4)

MATERIALS:

- Basswood Santa: small #2 size (1 ¾" x 3 ⅝", or 44mm x 92mm). For a bigger house, use a large #1 size (3 ½" x 5 ¾", or 89mm x 14.6cm) and photocopy the patterns at 200%.
- Graphite paper (optional)
- Paint: white (1), lavender (1), bright yellow (3), metallic gold (4), white (1), bright red (3), deep periwinkle (1), hunter green (4)
- Varnish: matte

TOOLS:

- Carving knife
- Woodburner with writing tip
- Pencil
- Paintbrush
- Awl

PATTERNS

Happy Holidays

Tip: *You can use the same pattern to make the panda shown on the cover; just change the paint scheme. You can carve the heart or leave it off as you prefer. For either bear, use the woodburner to create the fur texture.*

Bear With Me

Painting Guide:

Eyes, nose, ears: Black (3)

Body: Brown (3)

Heart: Bright red (3)

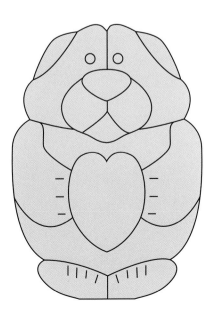

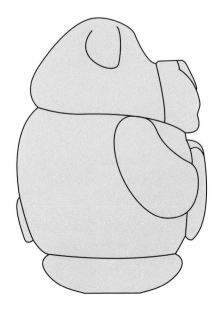

MATERIALS:

- Basswood egg: hen size
- Graphite paper (optional)
- Paint: black (3), brown (3), bright red (3)
- Varnish: matte

TOOLS:

- Carving knife
- Woodburner with writing tip
- Pencil
- Paintbrush

PAINT KEY

1 - Americana® Acrylics
2 - Apple Barrel® Colors
3 - Craft Smart® Acrylic
4 - Delta Ceramcoat® Acrylic

5 - FolkArt® Acrylic
6 - DecoArt® Crafter's Acrylic®
7 - FolkArt® Metallics
8 - DecoArt® Dazzling Metallics

PATTERNS

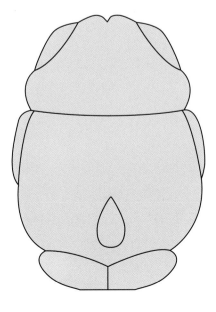

Leprechaun
WITH POT O' GOLD

Tip — *Use a micro V-tool to carve the leprechaun's beard and hair. Press a hollow hole circle punch into the top of the pot to mak[e] coins.*

Painting Guide:

Hatband, shoes, buttons, eyes: Black (3)

Hair, beard: Bright red (3)

Face, hands: Warm beige (1) mixed with red iron oxide (4)

Hat, clothes, shamrock on pot: Christmas green (2)

Vest stripes, shamrock: Apple tart green (3)

Buckles: Metallic silver (7)

Pants stripes: Dark yellow (3), red iron oxide (4)

Gold: Metallic gold (4)

Pot: Black (3)

Gold top coat: Glitter glue

MATERIALS:
- Basswood Santa: 2 each small #2 size (1 ¾" x 3 ⅝", or 44mm x 92mm)
- Graphite paper (optional)
- Paint: black (3), bright red (3), metallic gold (4), warm beige (1), Christmas green (2), apple tart green (3), metallic silver (7), dark yellow (3), red iron oxide (4)
- Glitter glue
- Varnish: matte

TOOLS:
- Carving knife
- Woodburner with writing tip
- Pencil
- Paintbrush

PAINT KEY

1 - Americana® Acrylics
2 - Apple Barrel® Colors
3 - Craft Smart® Acrylic
4 - Delta Ceramcoat® Acrylic
5 - FolkArt® Acrylic
6 - DecoArt® Crafter's Acrylic®
7 - FolkArt® Metallics
8 - DecoArt® Dazzling Metallics

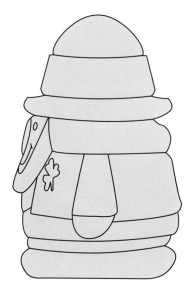

Easter Bunny

Painting Guide:

Eyes: Black (3)

Cheeks, feet, tail, box: White (1)

Body: Brown (3)

Bow: Lavender (1)

Peeps: Bright yellow (3)

Nose, ears: Red iron oxide (4) mixed with white (1)

MATERIALS:
- Basswood Santa: small #2 size (1 ¾" x 3 ⅝", or 44mm x 92mm)
- Graphite paper (optional)
- Paint: black (3), white (1), brown (3), lavender (1), bright yellow (3), red iron oxide (4)
- Varnish: matte

TOOLS:
- Carving knife
- Woodburner with writing tip
- Pencil
- Paintbrush

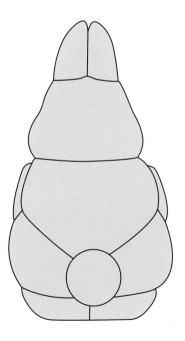

Uncle Sam

Painting Guide:

Eyes: Black (3)

Stripes, stars, vest: White (1)

Shoes: Brown (3)

Hands, face: Warm beige (1) mixed with red iron oxide (4)

Hat, coat: Navy blue (6)

Stripes, bow: Bright red (3)

Hair, beard: Metallic silver (7)

MATERIALS:

- Basswood Santa: small #2 size (1 ¾" x 3 ⅝", or 44mm x 92mm)
- Graphite paper (optional)
- Paint: black (3), white (1), brown (3), warm beige (1), navy blue (6), bright red (3) metallic silver (7), red iron oxide (4)
- Varnish: matte

TOOLS:

- Carving knife
- Micro (2mm) V-tool
- Woodburner with writing tip
- Pencil
- Paintbrush

PAINT KEY

1 - Americana® Acrylics
2 - Apple Barrel® Colors
3 - Craft Smart® Acrylic
4 - Delta Ceramcoat® Acrylic

5 - FolkArt® Acrylic
6 - DecoArt® Crafter's Acrylic®
7 - FolkArt® Metallics
8 - DecoArt® Dazzling Metallics

PATTERNS

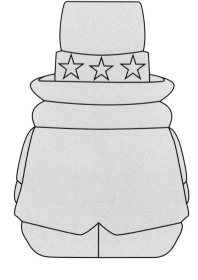

Tip: *Woodburn the feathers and paint them with a brown wash to let the details show through.*

Painting Guide:

Body: Brown (3)

Head, tail: White (1)

Eyes, beak, feet: Dark yellow (3)

Eyes: Black (3)

MATERIALS:

- Basswood egg: goose size
- Graphite paper (optional)
- Paint: white (1), brown (3), dark yellow (3), black (3)
- Varnish: matte

TOOLS:

- Carving knife
- Woodburner with writing tip
- Pencil
- Paintbrush

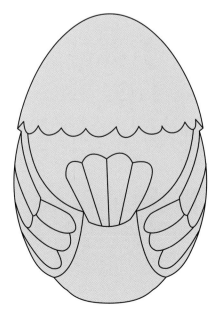

PATTERNS

Use a micro V-tool to carve the hair and hatband. Change the hair to make a boy or girl. Wrap black wire around a small dowel to make spirals. Use an awl to bore a small hole near the hat stem and glue the ends of the wires in place.

Trick-or-Treater

Painting Guide:

Hat, body: Pumpkin (4)

Hat leaves, stem: Hunter green (4)

Face, pumpkin face: Black (3)

Shoes: White (1)

Hands, face: Warm beige (1) mixed with red iron oxide (4)

Hair, shoes: Bright red (3)

MATERIALS:

- Basswood Santa: small #2 size (1 ¾" x 3 ⅝", or 44mm x 92mm)
- Graphite paper (optional)
- Paint: black (3), pumpkin (4), hunter green (4), white (1), warm beige (1), red iron oxide (4), bright red (3)
- Varnish: matte
- Dowel: scrap
- Wire: black
- Cyanoacrylate (CA) glue, such as Super Glue®

TOOLS:

- Carving knife
- Woodburner with writing tip
- Pencil
- Paintbrush
- Awl

PAINT KEY

1 - Americana® Acrylics
2 - Apple Barrel® Colors
3 - Craft Smart® Acrylic
4 - Delta Ceramcoat® Acrylic
5 - FolkArt® Acrylic
6 - DecoArt® Crafter's Acrylic®
7 - FolkArt® Metallics
8 - DecoArt® Dazzling Metallics

Vampire

Tip *Use the woodburner to texture the hair.*

Painting Guide:

Hair, cloak, clothes: Black (3)

Face, ears, vest, hands: White (1)

Cloak accents: Bright red (3)

MATERIALS:

- Basswood egg: hen size
- Graphite paper (optional)
- Paint: white (1), black (3), bright red (3)
- Varnish: matte

TOOLS:

- Carving knife
- Woodburner with writing tip
- Pencil
- Paintbrush

PAINT KEY

1 - Americana® Acrylics
2 - Apple Barrel® Colors
3 - Craft Smart® Acrylic
4 - Delta Ceramcoat® Acrylic
5 - FolkArt® Acrylic
6 - DecoArt® Crafter's Acrylic®
7 - FolkArt® Metallics
8 - DecoArt® Dazzling Metallics

PATTERNS

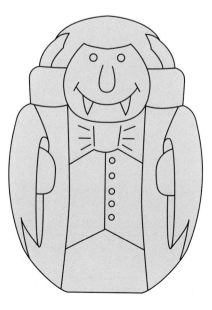

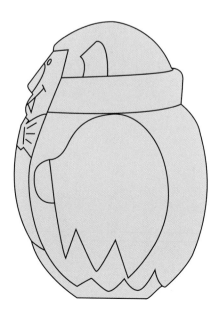

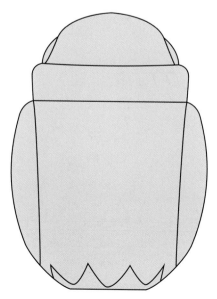

Frank

Use the woodburner to texture the hair.

Painting Guide:

Hair, pants, eyes, button: Black (3)

Face, hands: Apple tart green (3)

Shirt, shoes: Brown (3)

Eyes: Bright yellow (3)

Patch: Red iron oxide (4)

Bolts: Metallic silver (7)

MATERIALS:

- Basswood Santa: small #2 size (1 ¾" x 3 ⅝", or 44mm x 92mm)
- Graphite paper (optional)
- Paint: black (3), apple tart green (3), brown (3), bright yellow (3), red iron oxide (4), metallic silver (7)
- Varnish: matte

TOOLS:

- Carving knife
- Woodburner with writing tip
- Pencil
- Paintbrush

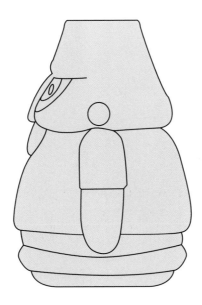

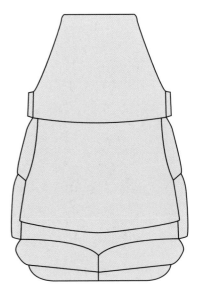

Wilma Witch

Tip **Carve the hair with the micro V-tool.**

Painting Guide:

Hat, hair, shoes: Black (3)

Tooth, stripes: White (1)

Stripes: Bright red (3)

Dress, hatband: Lavender (1)

Face, hands: Apple tart green (3)

MATERIALS:

- Basswood Santa: small #2 size (1 ¾" x 3 ⅝", or 44mm x 92mm). For a bigger witch, use a large #1 size (3 ½" x 5 ¾", or 89mm x 14.6cm) and photocopy the patterns at 200%.
- Graphite paper (optional)
- Paint: white (1), black (3), bright red (3), lavender (1), apple tart green (3)
- Varnish: matte

TOOLS:

- Carving knife
- Woodburner with writing tip
- Pencil
- Paintbrush

PAINT KEY

1 - Americana® Acrylics
2 - Apple Barrel® Colors
3 - Craft Smart® Acrylic
4 - Delta Ceramcoat® Acrylic
5 - FolkArt® Acrylic
6 - DecoArt® Crafter's Acrylic®
7 - FolkArt® Metallics
8 - DecoArt® Dazzling Metallics

PATTERNS

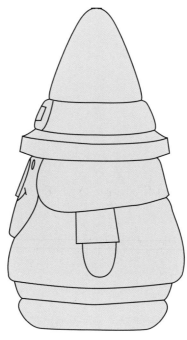

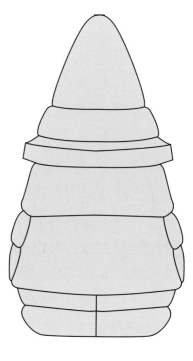

Press a hollow hole circle punch into the top of the cauldron to make bubbles.

Witch's Cauldron

Painting Guide:

Cauldron: Black (3)

Logs: Brown (3)

Potion accents: Christmas green (2), white (1)

Potion: Apple tart green (3)

Fire: Bright yellow (3)

Fire accents: Bright red (3), pumpkin (4)

MATERIALS:

- Basswood Santa: small #2 size (1 ¾" x 3 ⅝", or 44mm x 92mm). For a bigger cauldron, use a large #1 size (3 ½" x 5 ¾", or 89mm x 14.6cm) and photocopy the pattern at 200%.
- Graphite paper (optional)
- Paint: white (1), black (3), brown (3), Christmas green (2), apple tart green (3), bright yellow (3), bright red (3), pumpkin (4)
- Varnish: matte

TOOLS:

- Carving knife
- Woodburner with writing tip
- Hollow hole circle punch
- Pencil
- Paintbrush

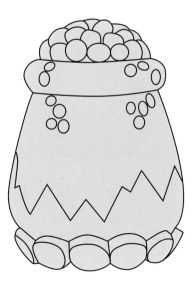

Black Cat

Tip *Turn the witch's familiar into a barn cat by painting one wit[h] orange and brown calico splotches.*

Painting Guide:

Body: Black (3)

Whiskers, claws: White (1)

Eyes: Apple tart green (3)

Nose, ears: White (1) mixed with red iron oxide (4)

MATERIALS:

- Basswood egg: pigeon size
- Graphite paper (optional)
- Paint: white (1), black (3), apple tart green (3), red iron oxide (4)
- Varnish: matte

TOOLS:

- Carving knife
- Woodburner with writing tip
- Pencil
- Paintbrush

PAINT KEY

1 - Americana® Acrylics
2 - Apple Barrel® Colors
3 - Craft Smart® Acrylic
4 - Delta Ceramcoat® Acrylic
5 - FolkArt® Acrylic
6 - DecoArt® Crafter's Acrylic®
7 - FolkArt® Metallics
8 - DecoArt® Dazzling Metallics

PATTERNS

Paint the whole owl white first, and then paint brown over the white to get the effect shown. Use a hen's egg to make a smaller owl for your farm set.

Owl

Painting Guide:

Belly, eyes, back of head: White (1)

Head, body, wings, belly feathers: Brown (3)

Beak, eyes: Dark yellow (3)

MATERIALS:

- Basswood egg: goose size
- Graphite paper (optional)
- Paint: white (1), brown (3), dark yellow (3)
- Varnish: matte

TOOLS:

- Carving knife
- Woodburner with writing tip
- Pencil
- Paintbrush

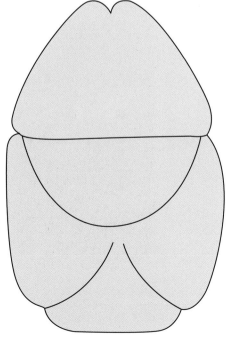

PATTERNS

Pumpkins

Tip *Wrap green wire around a small dowel to make spirals. Use an awl to bore a small hole near the stem and glue the ends of the wires in place. The pumpkins also go well with the farm and Thanksgiving pieces.*

Painting Guide:

Pumpkin: Pumpkin (4)

Leaves: Christmas green (2)

MATERIALS:

- Basswood egg: goose, hen, and pigeon sizes. For the hen egg, photocopy the pattern at 125%. For the goose egg, photocopy it at 175%.
- Graphite paper (optional)
- Paint: pumpkin (4), Christmas green (2)
- Varnish: matte
- Dowel: scrap
- Cyanoacrylate (CA) glue, such as Superglue®
- Floral wire: green

TOOLS:

- Carving knife
- Awl
- Pencil
- Paintbrush

PAINT KEY

1 - Americana® Acrylics
2 - Apple Barrel® Colors
3 - Craft Smart® Acrylic
4 - Delta Ceramcoat® Acrylic
5 - FolkArt® Acrylic
6 - DecoArt® Crafter's Acrylic®
7 - FolkArt® Metallics
8 - DecoArt® Dazzling Metallics

PATTERNS

PIGEON

HEN

GOOSE

Pumpkin House

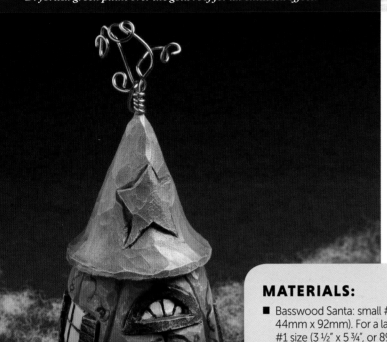

Painting Guide:

House: Pumpkin (4)

Drybrush accents: Black (3)

Door, trim:
Apple tart green (3)

Trim, drybrush roof:
Hunter green (4)

Windows: Bright yellow (3)

Roof: Metallic gold (4)

MATERIALS:

- Basswood Santa: small #2 size (1 ¾" x 3 ⅝", or 44mm x 92mm). For a larger house, use a large #1 size (3 ½" x 5 ¾", or 89mm x 14.6cm) and photocopy the patterns at 200%.
- Graphite paper (optional)
- Paint: black (3), pumpkin (4), apple tart green (3), hunter green (4), bright yellow (3), metallic gold (4)
- Varnish: matte
- Cyanoacrylate (CA) glue, such as Super Glue®
- Dowel: scrap

TOOLS:

- Carving knife
- Woodburner with writing tip
- Awl
- Pencil
- Paintbrush

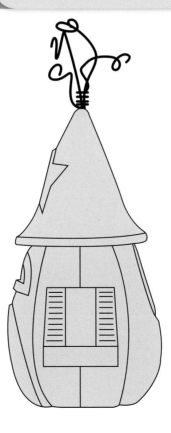

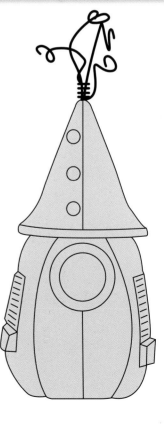

Be Thankful

Tip *Use a woodburner to make a feather texture.*

Painting Guide:

Hat, eyes: Black (3)

Head, tail: Dark chocolate (1)

Body: Brown (3)

Beak: Dark yellow (3)

Wattle: Bright red (3)

Buckle: Metallic silver (7)

MATERIALS:

- Basswood Santa: small #2 size (1 ¾" x 3 ⅝", or 44mm x 92mm)
- Graphite paper (optional)
- Paint: black (3), dark chocolate (1), brown (3), dark yellow (3), bright red (3), metallic silver (7)
- Varnish: matte

TOOLS:

- Carving knife
- Woodburner with writing tip
- Pencil
- Paintbrush

PAINT KEY

1 - Americana® Acrylics
2 - Apple Barrel® Colors
3 - Craft Smart® Acrylic
4 - Delta Ceramcoat® Acrylic
5 - FolkArt® Acrylic
6 - DecoArt® Crafter's Acrylic®
7 - FolkArt® Metallics
8 - DecoArt® Dazzling Metallics

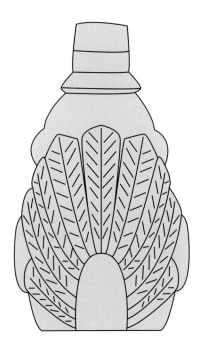

PATTERNS

Pilgrim Man

 Tip **Use a micro V-tool to texture the hair.**

Painting Guide:

Hat, shoes, belt: Black (3)

Collar, cuffs: White (1)

Jacket, hatband: Brown (3)

Pumpkin: Pumpkin (4)

Stem: Christmas green (2)

Face, hands: Warm beige (1) mixed with red iron oxide (4)

Buckle: Metallic silver (7)

Hair: Dark chocolate (1)

MATERIALS:

- Basswood Santa: small #2 size (1 ¾" x 3 ⅝", or 44mm x 92mm)
- Graphite paper (optional)
- Paint: white (1), black (3), brown (3), pumpkin (4), Christmas green (2), warm beige (1), metallic silver (7), dark chocolate (1), red iron oxide (4)
- Varnish: matte

TOOLS:

- Carving knife
- Woodburner with writing tip
- Micro (2mm) V-tool
- Pencil
- Paintbrush

 PAINT KEY

1 - Americana® Acrylics
2 - Apple Barrel® Colors
3 - Craft Smart® Acrylic
4 - Delta Ceramcoat® Acrylic

5 - FolkArt® Acrylic
6 - DecoArt® Crafter's Acrylic®
7 - FolkArt® Metallics
8 - DecoArt® Dazzling Metallics

PATTERNS

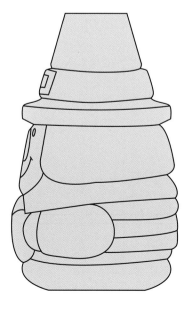
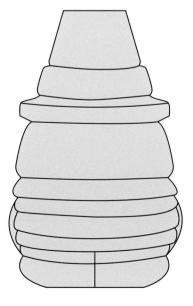

Pilgrim Woman

Painting Guide:

Shoes, eyes: Black (3)

Bonnet, collar, cuffs, apron: White (1)

Face, hands: Warm beige (1) mixed with red iron oxide (4)

Pie tin: Metallic silver (7)

Pie: Golden brown (3)

Dress: Brown (3)

MATERIALS:

- Basswood Santa: small #2 size (1 ¾" x 3 ⅝", or 44mm x 92mm)
- Graphite paper (optional)
- Paint: white (1), black (3), warm beige (1), red iron oxide (4), metallic silver (7), golden brown (3), brown (3)
- Varnish: matte

TOOLS:

- Carving knife
- Woodburner with writing tip
- Pencil
- Paintbrush

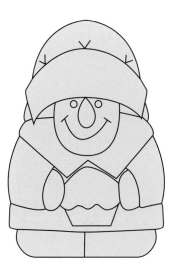

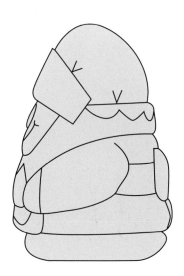

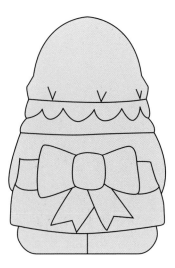

Native American Man

Tip *Texture the hair and add fringe to the coat and shoes with a woodburner.*

Painting Guide:

Clothing: Golden brown (3)

Face, hands: Warm beige (1) mixed with red iron oxide (4)

Corn: Dark yellow (3), red iron oxide (4), white (1)

Feather: White (1)

Headband, hair ties: Bright red (3)

Hair: Black (3)

MATERIALS:

- Basswood Santa: small #2 size (1 ¾" x 3 ⅝", or 44mm x 92mm)
- Graphite paper (optional)
- Paint: white (1), black (3), golden brown (3), warm beige (1), red iron oxide (4), dark yellow (3), bright red (3)
- Varnish: matte

TOOLS:

- Carving knife
- Woodburner with writing tip
- Pencil
- Paintbrush

PAINT KEY

1 - Americana® Acrylics
2 - Apple Barrel® Colors
3 - Craft Smart® Acrylic
4 - Delta Ceramcoat® Acrylic

5 - FolkArt® Acrylic
6 - DecoArt® Crafter's Acrylic®
7 - FolkArt® Metallics
8 - DecoArt® Dazzling Metallics

PATTERNS

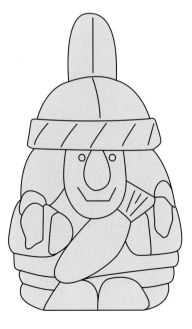

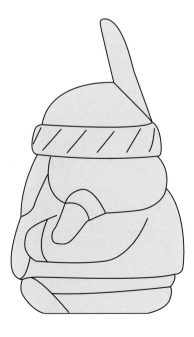

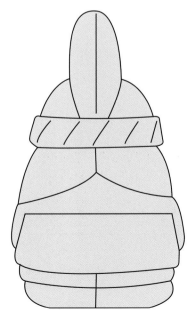

Native American Woman

Painting Guide:

Face, hands, baby face: Warm beige (1) mixed with red iron oxide (4)

Hair, baby hair: Black (3)

Headband, hair ties: Mediterranean blue (3)

Clothing: Golden brown (3)

Bandana: White (1)

Accents, baby mouth: Bright red (3)

Pumpkin: Pumpkin (4)

Leaves: Christmas green (2)

MATERIALS:

- Basswood Santa: small #2 size (1 ¾" x 3 ⅝", or 44mm x 92mm)
- Graphite paper (optional)
- Paint: white (1), black (3), warm beige, red iron oxide (4), Mediterranean blue (3), golden brown (3), bright red (3), pumpkin (4), Christmas green (2)
- Varnish: matte

TOOLS:

- Carving knife
- Woodburner with writing tip
- Pencil
- Paintbrush

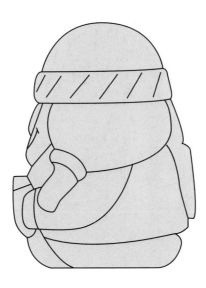
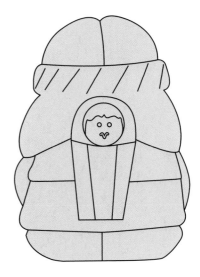

Monk with Basket of Plenty

Painting Guide:

Hood, robe: Brown (3)

Face, hands, toes: Warm beige (1) mixed with red iron oxide (4)

basket: Dark yellow (3)

Vegetables: Christmas green (2), pumpkin (4), bright red (3), lavender (1)

MATERIALS:
- Basswood Santa: small #2 size (1 ¾" x 3 ⅝", or 44mm x 92mm)
- Graphite paper (optional)
- Paint: brown (3), warm beige (1), red iron oxide (4), dark yellow (3), Christmas green (2), pumpkin (4), bright red (3), lavendar (1)
- Varnish: matte

TOOLS:
- Carving knife
- Woodburner with writing tip
- Pencil
- Paintbrush

PAINT KEY

1 - Americana® Acrylics
2 - Apple Barrel® Colors
3 - Craft Smart® Acrylic
4 - Delta Ceramcoat® Acrylic
5 - FolkArt® Acrylic
6 - DecoArt® Crafter's Acrylic®
7 - FolkArt® Metallics
8 - DecoArt® Dazzling Metallics

PATTERNS

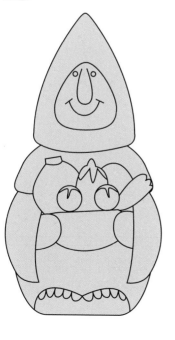
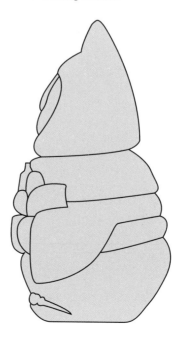
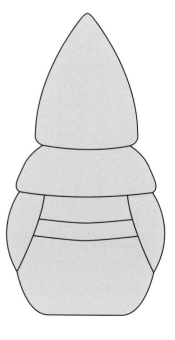

Painting Guide:

Eyes, smudges: Black (3)

Pants, accents: White (1)

Face, hands: Warm beige (1) mixed with red iron oxide (4)

Hair, ball: Brown (3)

Uniform: Bright red (3)

Helmet accents: Metallic silver (7)

MATERIALS:

- Basswood Santa: small #2 size (1 ¾" x 3 ⅝", or 44mm x 92mm)
- Graphite paper (optional)
- Paint: white (1), black (3), red iron oxide (4), warm beige (1), brown (3), bright red (3), metallic silver (7)
- Varnish: matte

TOOLS:

- Carving knife
- Woodburner with writing tip
- Pencil
- Paintbrush

PATTERNS

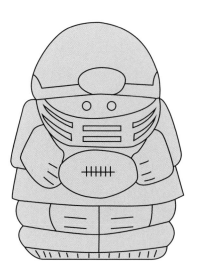

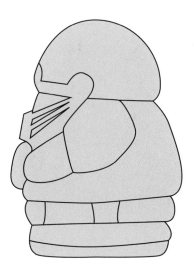

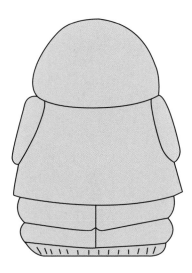

Use a micro (2mm) V-tool to carve the hatband.

Painting Guide:

Shoes, eyes: Black (3)

Face, hands: Warm beige (1) mixed with red iron oxide (4)

Hat, jacket: Bright red (3)

Hair: Brown (3)

Shoe accent: Metallic silver (7)

Scarf, pom-pom, mittens: White (1)

MATERIALS:

- Basswood Santa: small #2 size (1 ¾" x 3 ⅝", or 44mm x 92mm)
- Graphite paper (optional)
- Paint: white (1), black (3), warm beige (1), red iron oxide (4), bright red (3), metallic silver (7), brown (3)
- Varnish: matte

TOOLS:

- Carving knife
- Woodburner with writing tip
- Micro (2mm) V-tool
- Pencil
- Paintbrush

PAINT KEY

1 - Americana® Acrylics
2 - Apple Barrel® Colors
3 - Craft Smart® Acrylic
4 - Delta Ceramcoat® Acrylic
5 - FolkArt® Acrylic
6 - DecoArt® Crafter's Acrylic®
7 - FolkArt® Metallics
8 - DecoArt® Dazzling Metallics

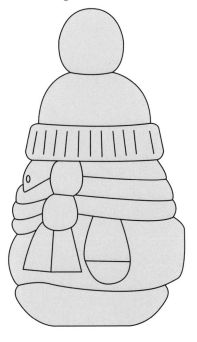

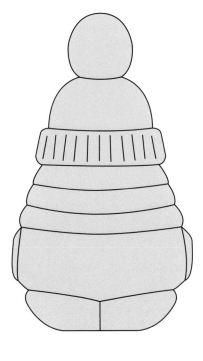

PATTERNS

Folk-Art Santa

Painting Guide:

Eyes: Black (3)

Beard, trim: White (1)

Hat, shirt: Bright red (3)

Jacket, patches: Mediterranean blue (3)

Face, hands: Warm beige (1) mixed with red iron oxide (4)

Mittens: Christmas green (2)

MATERIALS:

- Basswood egg: goose size
- Graphite paper (optional)
- Paint: white (1), black (3), warm beige (1), red iron oxide (4), bright red (3), Christmas green (2), Mediterranean blue (3)
- Varnish: matte

TOOLS:

- Carving knife
- Woodburner with writing tip
- Pencil
- Paintbrush

PAINT KEY

1 - Americana® Acrylics
2 - Apple Barrel® Colors
3 - Craft Smart® Acrylic
4 - Delta Ceramcoat® Acrylic
5 - FolkArt® Acrylic
6 - DecoArt® Crafter's Acrylic®
7 - FolkArt® Metallics
8 - DecoArt® Dazzling Metallics

PATTERNS

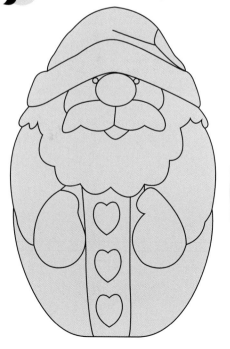

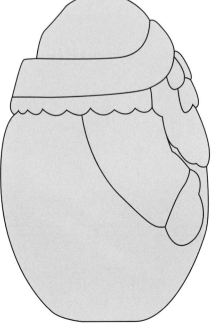

Mrs. Claus

Painting Guide:

Face, hands: Warm beige (1) mixed with red iron oxide (4)

Cap, trim: White (1)

Clothes, mouth: Bright red (3)

Eyes: Black (3)

Hair, brows: Metallic silver (7)

Mittens: Christmas green (2)

Glasses: Metallic gold (4), white (1)

MATERIALS:

- Basswood egg: hen size
- Graphite paper (optional)
- Paint: white (1), black (3), warm beige (1), red iron oxide (4), bright red (3), metallic gold (4), Metallic silver (7), Christmas green (2)
- Varnish: matte

TOOLS:

- Carving knife
- Micro (2mm) U-gouge
- Woodburner with writing tip
- Pencil
- Paintbrush

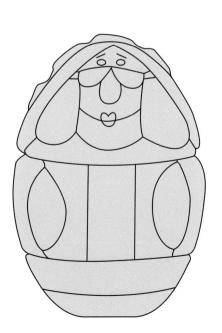

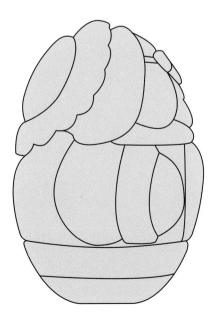

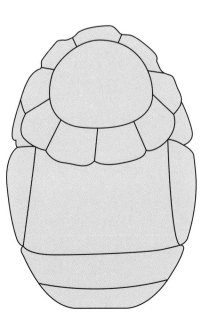

Reindeer

Painting Guide:

Eyes, hooves:
Black (3)

Body: Brown (3)

Collar, nose:
Bright red (3)

Bell: Metallic silver (7)

Antlers: Golden
brown (3)

MATERIALS:

- Basswood Santa: small #2 size
  (1 ¾" x 3 ⅝", or 44mm x 92mm)
- Graphite paper (optional)
- Paint: brown (3), black (3), bright
  red (3), metallic silver (7), golden
  brown (3)
- Varnish: matte

TOOLS:

- Carving knife
- Woodburner with writing tip
- Pencil
- Paintbrush

PAINT KEY

1 - Americana® Acrylics
2 - Apple Barrel® Colors
3 - Craft Smart® Acrylic
4 - Delta Ceramcoat® Acrylic
5 - FolkArt® Acrylic
6 - DecoArt® Crafter's Acrylic®
7 - FolkArt® Metallics
8 - DecoArt® Dazzling Metallics

PATTERNS

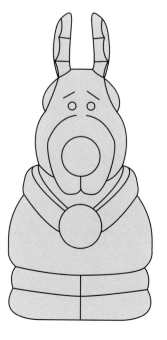

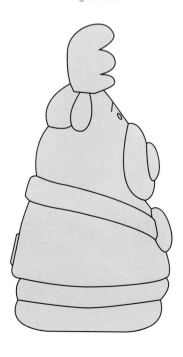

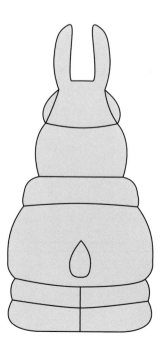

Elf

Painting Guide:

Belt, eyes: Black (3)

Beard, hair, stripes: White (1)

Hat, jacket, shoes: Christmas green (2)

Face, hands: Warm beige (1) mixed with red iron oxide (4)

Accents: Bright red (3)

Buckle, bells: Metallic silver (7)

MATERIALS:

- Basswood egg: pigeon size
- Graphite paper (optional)
- Paint: white (1), black (3), Christmas green (2), metallic silver (7), warm beige (1), bright red (3), red iron oxide (4)
- Varnish: matte

TOOLS:

- Carving knife
- Woodburner with writing tip
- Pencil
- Paintbrush

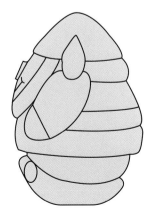

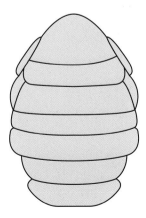

Tree

Tip **Use the micro V-tool for the details on the branches.**

Painting Guide:

Branches: Hunter green (4)

Drybrush accents: White (1)

MATERIALS:

- Basswood Santa: small #2 size (1 ¾" x 3 ⅝", or 44mm x 92mm)
- Graphite paper (optional)
- Paint: white (1), hunter green (4)
- Varnish: matte

TOOLS:

- Carving knife
- Woodburner with writing tip
- Micro (2mm) V-tool
- Pencil
- Paintbrush

PAINT KEY

1 - Americana® Acrylics
2 - Apple Barrel® Colors
3 - Craft Smart® Acrylic
4 - Delta Ceramcoat® Acrylic

5 - FolkArt® Acrylic
6 - DecoArt® Crafter's Acrylic®
7 - FolkArt® Metallics
8 - DecoArt® Dazzling Metallics

Nativity Set

MATERIALS:

- Basswood egg:
  1 per figure goose size
- Basswood block (baby in manger):
  1 ¼" x 2 ¼" x 3" (32mm x 57mm
  x 76mm)
- Graphite paper (optional)
- Paint: Mediterranean blue (3), brown
  (3), white (1), deep periwinkle (1),
  warm beige (1), red iron oxide (4),
  dark yellow (3), dark chocolate
  (1), pumpkin (4), black (3), metallic
  purple pearl (8), metallic royal ruby
  (8), metallic bronze (8), metallic dark
  patina green (8), metallic gold (4),
  apple tart green (3), Christmas
  green (2)
- Varnish: matte

TOOLS:

- Carving knife
- Woodburner with writing tip
- Pencil
- Paintbrush

Nativity Set

MARY

Painting Guide:

Robe: Mediterranean blue (3)

Face, hands: Warm beige (1) mixed with red iron oxide (4)

Hair: brown (3)

Robe trim: White (1)

Lips: red iron oxide (4)

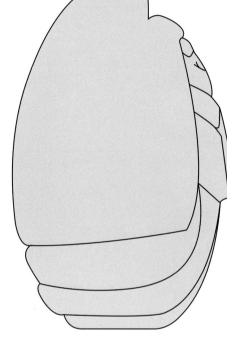

PATTERNS

JOSEPH

Painting Guide:

Beard: Brown (3)

Face, hands: Warm beige (1) mixed with red iron oxide (4)

Robe: Dark chocolate (1)

Head covering, stripes: White (1)

Accents: Pumpkin (4)

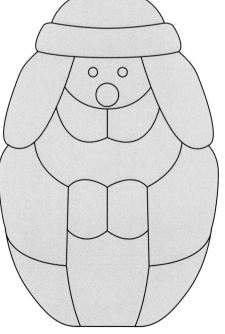
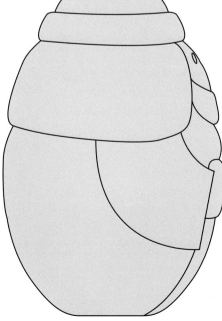

PATTERNS

Use a woodburner to carve wood texture in the manger.

Painting Guide:

Manger, hair: Brown (3)

Blanket: White (1)

Face: Warm beige (1) mixed with red iron oxide (4)

Lips: red iron oxide (4)

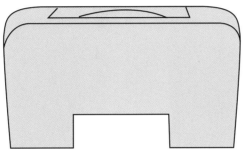

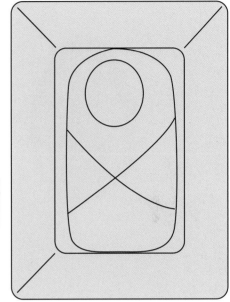

PATTERNS

Painting Guide:

Face, hands, sheep nose: Warm beige (1) mixed with red iron oxide (4)

Robe: Apple tart green (3)

Stripes, accents: Christmas green (2)

Head covering: Dark yellow (3)

Beard: Brown (3)

Sheep: White (1)

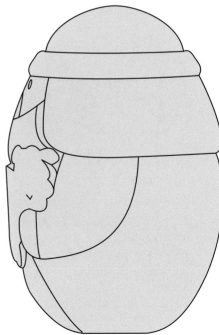

PATTERNS

Nativity Set

PAINT KEY

1 - Americana® Acrylics
2 - Apple Barrel® Colors
3 - Craft Smart® Acrylic
4 - Delta Ceramcoat® Acrylic

5 - FolkArt® Acrylic
6 - DecoArt® Crafter's Acrylic®
7 - FolkArt® Metallics
8 - DecoArt® Dazzling Metallics

ANGEL

Painting Guide:

Dress: Deep periwinkle (1)

Face, hands: Warm beige (1) mixed with red iron oxide (4)

Robe: White (1)

Hair: Dark yellow (3)

Wings, halo: Metallic gold (4)

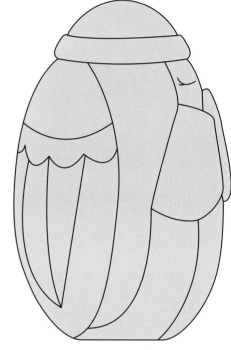

PATTERNS

KING #1

Painting Guide:

Face, hands: Warm beige (1) mixed with red iron oxide (4)

Hair: Black (3)

Robe: Metallic purple pearl (8)

Robe trim: Metallic royal ruby (8)

Shirt: Metallic bronze (8)

Crown, gift: Metallic gold (4)

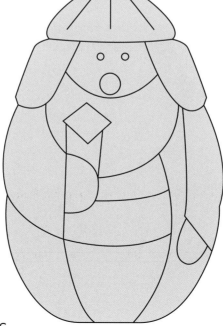
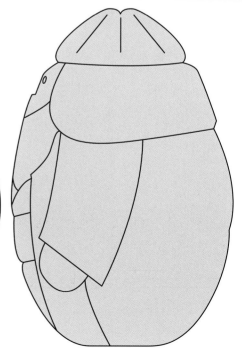

PATTERNS

Painting Guide:

Face, hands: Warm beige (1) mixed with red iron oxide (4)

Hair: Dark chocolate (1)

Robe: Metallic bronze (8)

Robe trim: Metallic dark patina green (8)

Crown, gift, stripes: Metallic gold (4)

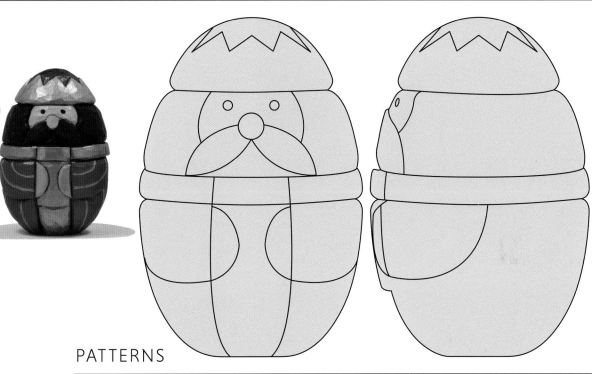

PATTERNS

Painting Guide:

Face, hands: Dark chocolate (1)

Beard: White (1)

Robe: Metallic royal ruby (8)

Robe trim: Metallic dark patina green (8)

Head covering: Metallic bronze (8)

Gift, trim accents: Metallic gold (4)

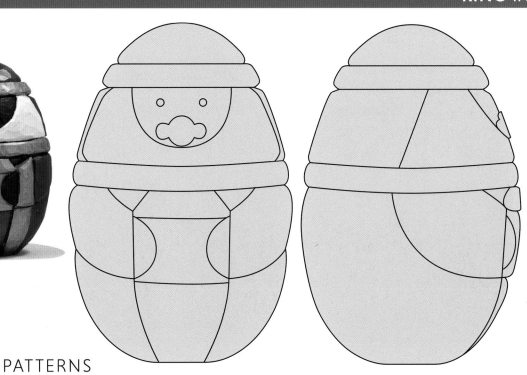

PATTERNS

MEET THE AUTHOR

I am often asked how I got into woodcarving. I am told that I don't fit folks' picture of an old guy who rocks on a porch and whittles a stick with a hound dog at his feet. My sister and I do many art shows each year, and we are usually the only woodcarvers there. I think we repeat the story of how we became carvers at least 20 times a show. We each

Lori Dickie

work on a project all day, and customers are fascinated to see woodcarvers in action. Also, they can see for themselves just how much work goes into the finished art that is displayed on our table.

It all started with our dad. Many years ago he took up woodcarving, and it turned out he had a real knack for it. My brother and sister, also talented artists, started carving, too. Because I was afraid of "playing with knives," I did not join in; at the time, I was working in clay. My dad and I participated in art shows together for years, with a lot of help from my mom. We spent the days selling our wares and arguing the question, is it more difficult to add material (clay) or remove material (carving) to make a character? Now that I have participated in the family tradition for 20 years, I think it is more challenging to take

away material to create a piece of art. (Not that I would ever have admitted that to my dad.)

After my dad passed away, my sister, Kristie, talked me into going to the local carving club so we could spend some sisterly time together. I agreed, but I was still nervous about using knives. The guys there were between the ages of 70 and 95, and most were retired. At first they were suspicious of two young women who showed up to carve at a senior center, but soon they collectively took us under their wing and we became "the sisters" for many years. They were wonderful. They showed a tremendous amount of patience and taught me the skills I use today, including how to sharpen my knife (and my sister's knives, because she never got the hang of it).

Lori with her husband, Steve.

Today, I am a professional woodcarver who has been carving for 20 years. I recently retired from a 39-year career as a budget administrator at the University of Michigan. In addition to the art shows I do with my sister, I am a member of Etsy, where I sell my carvings to collectors all over the world. I have three grown daughters, three sons-in-law, and two grandsons, with another one on the way. My husband, Steve, and I share a small hobby farm in Manchester, Michigan, with our three Rhodesian ridgebacks (large dogs). We grow vegetables and fruit, and raise chickens and turkeys for eggs and meat for our family and ourselves.

Please contact me at *Lmdickie1@etsy.com* or *Lmdickie@umich.edu*, or visit me online at *www.etsy.com/shop/lmdickie1*.

Lori and Steve with their family.

Lori and Steve live on a hobby farm, where they grow vegetables and fruit and raise chickens and turkeys.